Looking at SPAIN

RUPERT MARTIN

For many years Rupert Martin has been visiting Spain. He knows the country well – its summer heat and winter cold, the harsh mountains of the Pyrenees and the soft green country of the Atlantic coast; he knows too the fertile south, and the shores and islands of the Mediterranean sea.

In this book Rupert Martin writes about everyday life in Spain, the food and drink, the work of farmers and fishermen, the education of the children, the homes of the people and the rich life of street, market and café. He has a warm affection for the Spanish people and tells of the tough mountaineers of Aragon and Navarre, the graceful Andalusians, the lively Catalans and the proud people of Castile.

The book is magnificently illustrated with photographs in colour and black and white, many of them taken specially for this book.

Rupert Martin was for many years headmaster of a school in the west of England. Before that he was head of the British Council in Switzerland. A classical scholar and teacher of ancient history, he has journeyed extensively in Spain and Italy, and is the author of several successful books on European and Mediterranean countries, including *Looking at Italy* in this series.

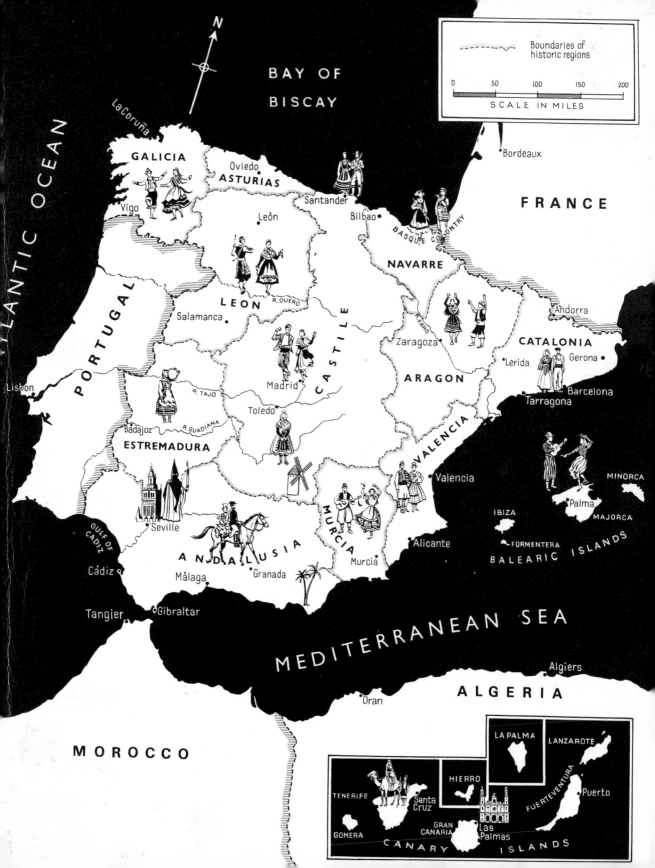

N

BAY OF
BISCAY

Boundaries of
historic regions

0   50   100   150   200
SCALE IN MILES

ATLANTIC OCEAN

La Coruña

GALICIA

Vigo

Oviedo
ASTURIAS

Santander

Bilbao

BASQUE COUNTRY

Bordeaux

FRANCE

León

NAVARRE

R. DUERO

Andorra

PORTUGAL

LEON

Salamanca

R. EBRO

Zaragoza

CATALONIA

Lerida   Gerona

Madrid

CASTILE

ARAGON

Barcelona

Tarragona

R. TAJO

Toledo

R. GUADIANA

Badajoz

ESTREMADURA

VALENCIA

Valencia

MINORCA

Palma

Lisbon

Seville

ANDALUSIA

MURCIA

Alicante

IBIZA

FORMENTERA

MAJORCA

BALEARIC ISLANDS

GULF OF CADIZ

Cádiz

Málaga   Granada

Murcia

Tangier   Gibraltar

MEDITERRANEAN SEA

Algiers

ALGERIA

Oran

MOROCCO

LA PALMA   LANZAROTE

HIERRO

TENERIFE   Santa
Cruz

FUERTEVENTURA

Puerto

GOMERA

GRAN
CANARIA

Las
Palmas

CANARY   ISLANDS

Looking at SPAIN

Young girls in *fiesta* dresses

Looking at

RUPERT MARTIN

Adam and Charles Black   London

J. B. Lippincott Company   Philadelphia and New York

Estepona on the Costa del Sol

SPAIN

Looking at Other Countries

Looking at HOLLAND   **Looking at NORWAY**
Looking at ITALY   **Looking at DENMARK**
Looking at GREECE   **Looking at JAPAN**

In preparation

Looking at FRANCE   **Looking at ISRAEL**

Grateful acknowledgement is made to the following for their permission to reproduce photographs:

Barnaby's Picture Library 1, 33b, 62a

Foto Ciganovic 27, 50a, 62b, 63a, b and c

Francis George 3, 10, 39a, 40a, 42, 50b and c, 51a and b

J. Allan Cash 5

Jonathan Rutland 6, 7, 8, 9, 11a and b, 13, 14, 15, 16, 17a and b, 18, 19, 20, 21, 22a and b, 23, 24, 25, 26, 28, 29, 30, 31, 32, 33a, 34, 35a, b and c, 41, 46, 47, 52, 54a and b, 55, 58, 59

Spanish National Tourist Office 12, 36a and b, 37, 40b, 44, 45, 48, 49, 56a and b, 57a and b, 60, 61

Tourist Photo Library 39b

The photographs on the cover are by Foto Ciganovic

The endpaper maps are by H. Johns

2/943

SBN 7136 1018 2
© 1969   A. & C. Black Ltd   4, 5 & 6 Soho Square   London W1V 6AD
Library of Congress Catalog Card Number: 73-78938

PRINTED IN GREAT BRITAIN BY *JARROLD & SONS LTD.* NORWICH

CONTENTS

Drinking from a *porón*

Berdun, a hilltop town

The Country

Spain juts out from the southwest corner of Europe, and is separated from France by the Pyrenees range of mountains. Because it is cut off like this Spain is sometimes called 'the unknown country of Europe'. Spain and Portugal together form the Iberian Peninsula, named for the ancient inhabitants of this region. The Romans called Portugal 'Lusitania', and the whole peninsula 'the bull's hide' from its shape.

Spain is made up of a huge mass of rock which lies between high mountain ranges. This central plateau is called the *meseta*, or little table, and from all sides the roads climb steeply up to it, making travel slow and difficult. Everywhere there are jagged ranges of mountains called *sierra* (Spanish for saw), and the roads have to follow their ridges and valleys.

In summer the *meseta* is burnt brown by the blistering sun, and at other seasons it is ravaged by an icy wind. Its climate has

6

been described as 'nine months winter and three months hell'. It is not surprising that most large cities – except the capital, Madrid – lie off the *meseta*, either near the coast or in the fertile courses of the rivers.

Founded by Philip II, Madrid, in the middle of the country, is well placed for a capital, and today the great Spanish highways radiate like spokes from a wheel with its hub in Madrid. It is almost impossible to travel from the north to the south of Spain without passing through Madrid. Equally, a *Madrileño*, in a long day's drive from his home, can encounter either the wild gales of La Coruña in the northwest or the fiery heat of Seville in the south.

Northeast Spain is dominated by the Pyrenees, a mass of hills and high peaks, which extend for 260 miles from the Bay of Biscay to the Mediterranean. Their slopes are tawny, sombre and barren, with few inhabitants, and in places they straggle nearly seventy miles into Spain.

The *sierra* above Pancorbo

Ricefields near Valencia

The Pyrenees slope sharply on the French side and gently on the Spanish. This makes transport easier for the French because their roads can run at the foot of the range, but difficult for the Spanish who have to negotiate high ribs of rock jutting out from the central massif.

Nestling among the Pyrenees is the tiny, mountainous state of Andorra. This ancient haunt of smugglers is nominally independent, but it acknowledges the joint overlordship of the President of France and the Spanish Bishop of Urgel.

The other three main mountain regions in Spain are all on a smaller scale than the Pyrenees. The district of Asturias in the north is wild, savage and remote. The Sierra Morena, the 'dark range', acts as a steep rampart between central and southern Spain. The third group, the Sierra Nevada, the 'snowy range', rises to 11,000 feet above the semi-tropical scenery of the south. Here you can ski and swim within a few hours on the same day.

The Mediterranean coast of Spain is 900 miles long from the French frontier to Gibraltar. Near Barcelona lies the Costa

RIGHT Fishing boats at Tarifa, the southernmost point of Spain. The mountains of North Africa can be seen in the distance

Brava, the 'rugged shore', a crowded holiday playground, fringed by miles of pine trees, red rocks and blue bays. Barcelona, the great rival to Madrid, is Spain's chief seaport and commercial capital. Here the spirited Catalans provide the hustle and bustle which is lacking in the dignified Castilian cities of the *meseta*. Farther south lie the orange groves of Valencia, and beyond this the sun-drenched province of Andalusia. Here, only nine miles from Africa across the Strait of Gibraltar, invading Moors entered Spain in A.D. 711 and dominated the country for nearly eight centuries. Today many of the low, white houses still reflect Moorish influence. Throughout Andalusia there are traces of Phoenician, Greek, Roman and Arab merchants and conquerors who have left behind them successive layers of dwellings through the years.

Córdoba with the river Guadalquivir in spate

West of Gibraltar lies the port of Cádiz and the town of Jerez (from which we get the word sherry), surrounded by its vineyards. Here also flows the 'Great River', Guadalquivir, on which the sixteenth-century Spanish galleons sailed up to Seville loaded with Aztec and Inca treasures from Mexico and Peru. The valley of the Guadalquivir provides one of the most fertile areas of Spain and here, in ancient times, was the city of Tarshish, mentioned in the Bible.

The historic cities of Córdoba and Granada are in Andalusia. The former has a Christian cathedral built inside the walls of a huge Moorish mosque. Granada is overlooked by the red-brown bulk of the Alhambra palace, also built by the Moors.

The Atlantic coast of Spain is much shorter than the Mediterranean one (from the French border to La Coruña in the northwest is less than 500 miles) and it is completely different in character. Here are no signs of the long, dry burning heat of the south, no dust-smothered roads, no vividly blazing landscapes. Instead there are gentle hills, green with trees and an average rainfall of 66 inches compared with about ten in the south.

The western part of Spain, adjoining Portugal, and separated by it from the sea, is rocky and bleak. In this 'extreme land' as the Spanish call it, many of the New World explorers were born, among them Cortés and Pizarro, and were driven forth by the barren character of their native soil to seek new and richer homes overseas. This is still the most backward province of Spain. For centuries it was a sort of no-man's-land, first between Christians and Moors, later between Spain and Portugal.

Spain is officially divided into 50 provinces (including the Balearic and Canary Islands) for the purpose of government. But the names of larger divisions are still also freely used, such as Castile, Aragon and Navarre, recalling proud and ancient kingdoms – now vanished – which had their own languages and customs.

Physically, Spain is not a beautiful country. Except in the Pyrenean valleys and in the north, trees and even shrubs are rare. Grass is parched for many months, and wheat has only a brief season. Beauty is found in less obvious ways – in the strange clarity of the atmosphere, in specks of cloud poised above a sky of flawless blue, in groups of brown huts clustered like beehives on bare hillsides. There are no half-tones in the Spanish scene, no misty outlines, only the hard, fierce light of her tireless sun.

A farmhouse and olive groves, not far from Toledo

The Sierra de Aralrar in northern Spain

An old man of Estremadura

People and Homes

Spaniards are as varied as their climate. There are more sharply marked divisions of regional feeling in Spain than anywhere else in Europe. The main distinction is between Castilians and Catalans, whose dialects vary considerably. Castilians are mostly lean, dark, sombre, dignified people, whose speech is held to be the purest form of Spanish. They are apt to appear grave, reserved and taciturn. Catalans are more lively, inventive, restless and energetic. They often have a revolutionary outlook and are impatient of decrees from the central government in Madrid.

The Basques who live in the angle between the Atlantic coast and the Pyrenees claim to be the most ancient race on earth. They speak a language which appears to the stranger full of x's and z's and other tongue-twisters. The men of 'rock-ribbed Aragón', in the Pyrenees, have a reputation for courage and obstinacy – it is said that they can knock nails in with their heads.

The Galicians in the northwest corner are tough, hardy folk, nurtured in a fierce climate. General Francisco Franco, who became head of the Spanish state in 1939, was born and brought up in Galicia.

The Andalusians of the far south are more easy-going. Here the sun is hot, and crops seem to grow well enough without much care. From the south came the legend of *mañana* (Let's put it off till tomorrow!). This is often true only in that the Spaniard refuses to be hurried and will always elect to do things in his own time.

Despite the variety of types, certain things are true of Spaniards all over the land. They are polite and they are hospitable to strangers. They are cruel in some ways, but very kind in others, especially to children, whom they adore. They are proud of their *hidalguería*, the ancient idea of chivalry (the word *hidalgo* means 'lower nobility'). This pride is by no means confined to the upper classes. Everyone takes great care of his appearance, and no one in Spain would dream of pottering about in old clothes during his leisure hours. Bootblacks abound everywhere, and shoes must present the gloss which used to mark a gentleman who was accustomed to riding on horseback while menial people trod the dusty roads.

Bootblacks in the Ramblas, Barcelona

Maria Luisa park, Seville

This feeling also explains the unpunctuality which is wide-spread in Spain. A *caballero* (gentleman) does not deign to worry about time-keeping. This (and the climate) accounts for the late hour of meals in Spain. The midday meal usually starts at about two o'clock and often goes on till four. It is very difficult to dine anywhere before nine-thirty in the evening, and few places of entertainment open before eleven o'clock.

After lunch almost everyone has a *siesta*. All activities come to a halt for two or three hours, and Spain comes to life again only around six in the evening. If a stranger happens to be abroad during the *siesta* he will catch glimpses of people asleep under a tree or a wall, in any shelter they can find from the fierce heat of the sun.

Between six and eight o'clock in the evening is the time of the *paseo*. In this evening parade women and girls stroll together in groups meeting men and boys in other groups, passing each other with glances and smiles. This promenade is watched from the small tables outside cafés which are full of people drinking sherry and nibbling cheese or shellfish. Entertaining among Spaniards is almost always done at these cafés, partly because the standard of their homes is often poorer than respect for 'fine appearance' requires. Spain is one of the most difficult countries in the world for a casual stranger to be invited into the home. In these cafés takes place also the evening *tertulia*, which is a meeting among cronies to discuss and debate every subject under the sun, from bull fighting to politics. Only the very prosperous open their houses to give parties.

Many rich and noble people in Spain are still extremely clannish. They have long and complicated names, derived from both their mother's and father's families. There is much formality of address, and courtesy often requires the use of the title *Don* for a man and *Doña* for a lady, used before the Christian name. These terms used to be given to the nobility only, but politeness has now extended them widely. It was once customary for all young girls to be very strictly chaperoned (especially in the south, owing to the Moorish influence). This practice has now almost died out, especially in big cities where the influx of tourists has brought a wind of change to many formerly strict habits. Never before have old Spanish traditions been exposed to so many new influences from abroad.

The evening *tertulia*

The homes of Spanish people vary as much as their land and their climate. In the north the houses are solid and adapted to a temperate climate. Many of them have a *mirador*, a projecting balcony, glassed in on three sides, where the family can sit in the sun, protected from cold winds. As a result, if you look at the houses of La Coruña from the sea you appear to be gazing on a great wall of glass, which turns to a flaming red as it catches the rays of the setting sun.

In the south houses are almost African in character, owing to their history as much as to their latitude. All over Andalusia life is lived largely out of doors, in a benign climate, and the courtyard rather than the hearth is the centre of the home.

Spanish people, with their exquisite courtesy, always say to anyone entering, '*Nuestra casa es su casa*' – 'Our house is your house' – but in practice it is only close members of the family who regularly gain acceptance in the home. Life within the Spanish family is very sociable, and they love living in a crowd, with plenty of noise. Living is much cheaper when several generations pile into the same apartment, and Spain is not a rich country. Many Spaniards have large families, and it is a struggle for the parents to bring them up, though

A street in
Almonte

most big firms have schemes to benefit workers with numerous children.

All ranks in Spain are devoted to their *niños* (children). Whole families love to make expeditions together, perhaps to see a member of the clan off on a train journey. Even at midnight you will see grandparents and tiny grandchildren gathered at the station, shouting, singing, gesticulating, even weeping if the parting is to be a long one.

In many domestic ways Spain still has an old-fashioned look. Much cooking is still done with charcoal, even in houses which have electricity. Women in the country still wash their clothes in the river, and, mainly in the towns, the *sereno*, the nightwatchman, still patrols the streets to deter thieves and unlocks the outer door of your dwelling with a giant key when you return home in the small hours of the morning.

Most Spanish children are called after saints, and it is on the name day of their saint rather than on their birthdays that they have parties and receive presents. The other chief time for gift giving is not Christmas but Epiphany (January 6) when the Three Kings visit all houses and fill the shoes which the *niños* have tied to their balconies. Many grown-ups also exchange presents at Epiphany which is the season for rewarding those who have served you well, like Boxing Day in Britain.

Spanish coins. Five *pesetas* will buy a cup of coffee

Food and Drink

The art of cooking in Spain is as varied as the food itself, for the south favours food fried in olive oil, the midlands like roast food and the north prefers stews.

Spain's most famous dish is called *paella*. Its true home is Valencia, but every region has its own variant. The basis of *paella* is rice, tinted to a warm crocus shade with saffron, to which an astonishing selection of ingredients is added – chicken, ham, veal, liver, tomato, pimento, green peas, small beans and, in one version, shellfish. Paella should always be served from the pan in which it has been cooked, and it should be sufficiently dry for the grains of rice to fall apart when it is served.

Cooking *paella*

Roast suckling pig is a great delicacy in Castile, and all over Spain *chorizo*, a red peppery sausage, is eaten. Andalusia has a special soup, *gazpacho*, so good that it has now spread to all regions. It has a base of oil and vinegar in which are chopped tomato, garlic, cucumber, onion, green pepper and breadcrumbs. In hot weather *gazpacho* is served ice cold and is usually garnished with *mayonnaise* (named after Mahón, the capital of Minorca in the Balearic Islands, where it was invented).

Vegetables have a short season in Spain. They are delicious while they last, but the hot sun brings them to maturity early in the year and shrivels them up quickly. Fruit is abundant everywhere. In the south you see golden mounds of oranges and huge pyramids of green watermelons. Spain is renowned for shellfish of every type. The shrimps, prawns, crabs and crayfish are used to form the little titbits called *tapas* which are always offered in Spanish cafés and bars with the evening drink – a necessary snack in a land where breakfast and lunch are very light meals and dinner is served much later than in the rest of Europe.

Many wines and brandies are made in Spain, apart from the sherry for which she is famous, and which is sometimes served in very hot weather with ice and even orange juice. Normally it is drunk as an aperitif. Wine is often drunk from a *porón* – a glass vessel with a thin spout which directs a jet of wine into the drinker's mouth – but some skill is needed to do this successfully. There is a photograph of a porón on the Contents page.

Madrid

Madrid, standing on its plateau, is the highest capital in Europe, more than 2,000 feet above sea level. In the magnificent days of the Hapsburg monarchy, in the sixteenth and seventeenth centuries, it used to be said that 'the throne of the King of Spain stands next to the throne of God' – in a double sense.

To the Spaniards Madrid is a new city. Toledo, 40 miles to the south, has the air of ancient grandeur the capital lacks. Madrid was quite a humble town until King Philip II moved his court there from Toledo in 1560. Now, with nearly three million inhabitants, it is the largest city in Spain, rivalled only by Barcelona with nearly two million, but it is worth notice that the largest Spanish speaking cities in the world are not in Spain. Most of South and all of Latin America speak Spanish; Buenos Aires and Mexico City are both considerably bigger than any city in Spain.

In modern Madrid new buildings dominate the old. Huge skyscraper hotels have been built in recent years, and the busy streets are full of shining cars. Parks, avenues and promenades are well laid out, and signs of prosperity are visible everywhere. There is hardly a trace now of the widespread destruction which the city suffered in the Civil War of 1936–1939. On the outskirts a fine new suburb has been built to house the university which attracts students from all over the world. Madrid is rich in parks with trees, lawns, flowerbeds and fountains to give relief from the burning midsummer sun.

It is pleasant to wander round the ancient quarters of Madrid. Here you will find quiet squares, such as the Plaza Mayor, whose stately houses are decorated with iron balconies where noblemen used to gather to watch jousts and bull fights.

The Prado gallery contains one of the finest picture collections in the world. Famous artists from every land are represented, but particularly the Spanish masters. Here Velásquez has mirrored the court of his royal patron, Philip IV, in magic tones of light and shadow. Here the terrifying paintings of Goya show the horrors of war and devastation during the period when the Spanish and British were fighting the French, and the Duke of Wellington was campaigning against Napoleon's marshals across Portugal and Spain.

Another form of art is represented by a charming statue of Don Quixote and Sancho Panza. Cervantes, one of the earliest novelists, wrote their story to mock many of the absurdities which had grown up in the age of chivalry and in so doing created a monument of humanity's brave striving in the face of dangers. It is a true reflection of the Spaniard's undaunted courage.

The Royal Palace in Madrid, perched above the little river Manzanares, has been left just as it was when King Alfonso XIII went into exile in 1931. Much has happened since then.

Retiro park, Madrid

The market of El Rastro   The Escorial palace

A period of republican government was followed by the Civil War which was ended when General Francisco Franco became the head of state.

The palace houses a wonderful series of tapestries, mostly Flemish, showing scenes from legend and history. The Royal Armoury in one part of the palace houses a magnificent collection of arms and armour, displayed on dummy figures in the most lifelike way.

Near the Plaza Mayor you will find, amid crooked lanes and red-tiled roofs, El Rastro, the Old Market, where you may be lucky enough to pick up amazing bargains for a tiny sum. Its stalls are loaded with books, clocks, guitars, castanets, pictures and all sorts of fantastic oddments.

Thirty miles north of Madrid, at the foot of the Guadarrama mountains, stands the granite mass of the Escorial palace, built by Philip II in memory of his father, Charles V. Dedicated to St Lorenzo it is designed in the shape of the gridiron on which that saint was roasted. This vast building has miles of corridors, 300 rooms and nearly 3,000 windows. Here is the burial place of the Spanish royal family. Kings and queens lie ranged on shelves in a gloomy vault of black marble decorated with bronze. Here King Philip lived the life of a poor hermit, while, at the same time, he controlled the greatest power of his age. Sitting at a desk in El Escorial he drew up the plans for his luckless Armada which suffered defeat and shipwreck off the coasts of Britain in 1588.

A magnificent road-tunnel now runs under the Guadarrama mountains, leading north from El Escorial to Segovia. Here a mighty aqueduct, built in the time of the Roman emperor Trajan, spans the city, dwarfing the houses and taverns which cluster beneath it.

The best sights in Madrid are the *Madrileños* themselves. At a busy hour the hum of their chatter is deafening, punctuated by the cries of lottery ticket sellers and street vendors. You see small boys in narrow alleys swinging their cloaks playing *toreros*. You see legions of shrill children walking with their nurses in the huge Retiro park which covers a large area of the capital. You see, sometimes even in fashionable quarters, the countryman who has strayed there with his donkey, crying his wares amid the bustle of traffic. All is noise and energy, until the time of the *siesta*, when suddenly a hush falls until the sun sinks and Madrid resumes its vivid life in the cool of the evening.

The Roman aqueduct at Segovia. No clamps or mortar were used in its construction

Barcelona and the Costa Brava

Barcelona is the second largest, and quite the most lively, Spanish city. It ranks with Marseilles, Genoa and Naples as a great Mediterranean port. Barcelona is the capital of the Catalan people, age-old rivals of the Castilians. It is the traditional home of new ideas and new movements, often bitterly opposed to the strict control which the Church keeps on the lives of most Spaniards. It was here that anti-Franco feeling was strongest in the Civil War of 1936–1939, when large parts of the city were destroyed by bombardment. Barcelona has always been the most cosmopolitan of Spanish cities, looking outward to the Mediterranean rather than inward to the *meseta*.

Above the harbour towers a high column with a statue of Columbus, symbol of Barcelona's traffic with the sea. Nearby is a full-scale model of his flagship, *Santa Maria* (see page 47). To this city Columbus returned after the historic voyage to the West, with a train of Indians bearing gold and parrots and strange fruits, to confound the scoffers who had laughed at him for a wild, crazy dreamer. His spirit of adventure and discovery is still abroad in Barcelona, whose docks are filled with merchant ships, serving the factories, mills, tanneries and locomotive works which teem on the outskirts of this ever-growing port.

The Columbus monument, Barcelona

The hub of the city's life is the *Plaza de Cataluña*. From this grand square down to the harbour runs a mile-long series of wide, tree-shaded streets, called collectively the Ramblas. This is the most striking sight in Barcelona. Here is a market by day and a parade by night, unique for noise, glitter and gaiety. All along the Ramblas stalls are crammed with flowers, fruit, fish, caged birds and pets of every kind. Here you can buy the vast bunches of blooms with which Spanish people salute their friends on all occasions of joy or sorrow. Here they stroll till the early hours of the morning, clad in their best clothes, exchanging greetings and gossip, pausing at intervals among the cafés and newspaper kiosks which abound.

The Ramblas are also the special home of the sellers of lottery tickets who throng the streets of Spanish cities. The price of tickets is divisible into tenths, hundredths and even thousandths, so that all can buy, however poor. Occasionally the winning number is held by some small village where most of the inhabitants have bought a tiny fraction of a ticket, and all take part in the share-out and rejoicing. The sale of lottery tickets is often entrusted to handicapped people who cannot do other work.

A lottery ticket seller

Plaza de Cataluña, Barcelona

Near the Ramblas also stand the booths of another public service – the professional letter-writer, called the *memorialista*. Many Spaniards, particularly the elderly from remote regions, find writing beyond their powers, so they hire these experts to put their words on paper. Often farmers' letters are written in this fashion, and a brisk trade is done also in love letters. The young man or woman sits in a little box opposite the scribe and declaims his or her feelings which are then written down with suitable ardour. Sometimes the traffic is in angry letters to troublesome adversaries, when the *memorialista* is asked to suggest any rude words which the speaker may have omitted.

The vast size of Barcelona can well be seen from the heights of Tibidabo behind the city. Legend declares that when the

Devil took Christ to a high point to show Him all the kingdoms of the earth he said 'Tibi dabo' (I will give to thee) in return for His obedience. It is certainly a view of astounding scope. From Tibidabo you can look directly down on the graceful avenues, the huddle of the ancient city near the cathedral, the busy quaysides of the port, and the bustling traffic of a huge modern city.

One sight not to be missed in Barcelona is the Spanish Village. It contains replicas in stone of the various styles of building throughout Spain, illustrating their different regional forms. In addition, this 'village' is peopled with craftsmen from these districts, working at their own trades and selling their handicrafts. The chief interest of the village is that it is solid and genuine, not a shoddy collection of faked models. It was originally constructed for a big exhibition in 1929, but proved so popular that it has become a permanent feature of Barcelona.

Barcelona has been the home of many revolutionary artists. Pablo Picasso grew up there. In the early years of this century he helped to create the revolt against the rigid rules which had bound painters till then. His Cubist pictures have led the way to other and more daring new forms of art. Salvador Dali is another Catalan. In his canvases we see strange combinations of bizarre figures, skeletons, twisted trees and machines. Dali deliberately set out to 'paint like a madman'. But at the same time he displays in his crazy designs all the care and skill of an ancient master.

Dancing the *sardana* in front of the cathedral

The Spanish Village

Antonio Gaudi led a similar revolution in architecture. An unfinished church designed by him stands in Barcelona, dedicated to the Holy Family. The building looks like a forest run mad, with a tangle of streamers, trees, flowers and other objects all moulded from stone, but looking as if they must be made of some soft material.

In the mountains behind Barcelona stands the great monastery of Monserrat. Thousands of pilgrims visit it every year, to hear the celebrated chanting of its Benedictine monks and to pay homage to the Black Virgin enthroned there. This image is said to have been brought there by St Peter twenty years after the Crucifixion. It was buried for safety when the Moors first invaded Spain, and it miraculously revealed its hiding place to some poor shepherds on a hillside many years later.

Barcelona is also a port of embarkation for the Balearic Islands. Sixteen of these are inhabited but only three are well-known – Majorca, Minorca and Ibiza. These islands were the lairs of pirates for many centuries. Now they have half a million inhabitants, and Palma, the capital, is a considerable city, with a flourishing tourist trade.

The Mediterranean coast on both sides of Barcelona has been developed with astonishing speed in the past twenty years. Camping colonies among the pines and sand dunes are scattered between new seaside towns whose buildings have been run up fast, with cheap labour and materials. There is no need to spend money on elaborate heating systems in this normally mild climate. Sunseekers from all the lands of northern Europe flock to these shores throughout the months of summer. Forty miles northwest of Barcelona the Costa Brava begins. Part of its popularity as a holiday haunt is the fact that no direct road can run along the coast. The shore is far too broken and indented. Very rough and narrow roads run down to it from inland towns such as Gerona, through lines of cork and eucalyptus trees and hills of scrub and twisted umbrella pines. These tracks end in small bays or fishing villages, once ravaged by Barbarossa and his corsairs; now given over to underwater swimming and all the activities of a seaside holiday. The nearness of the Pyrenees guarantees cooling breezes to temper the southern sun. The blueness and translucence of its tiny bays have made the Costa Brava world famous.

Tossa del Mar on the Costa Brava

Toledo

Toledo is perched upon a rock, high above the river Tagus, with its waters running in a loop far below. Two long bridges link the city with the country outside, which is bare and bleak and brown. Above the roofs of the city tower the cathedral and the castle, scene of a famous siege in the Civil War.

Toledo is a maze of narrow, cobbled streets of dark houses. Sometimes among these you will find a little *plaza*, where women gossip as they fill their water jars from a well. Most of the transport in these tiny lanes is by donkey, as it is in many Spanish cities. From its twisting streets you catch glimpses of brightly tiled, flower-decorated courtyards in the shadows behind huge outer doors. Many of the finest buildings in Toledo are adorned with the typically Moorish tiles called *azulejos*, which are still manufactured and used for indoor decoration in present-day Spain. Three old gateways lead into Toledo. One of these, the Gate of the Sun, has graceful Moorish arches flanked by turrets which glisten in the sunset.

In ancient times Toledo was celebrated for its swordmakers. Their finely tempered blades, the best in the world, could be bent in a circle until the point touched the hilt. Here the Moors introduced the graceful art of damascening (named from

Damascus) the hilts and scabbards, by beating threads of gold and silver into the metal. The modern method is to cut a pattern, and then rub a black pigment over it – less attractive but much cheaper. In a world which has few uses for swords, the smiths of Toledo have turned to a huge trade in scissors, knives and other steel objects, still tempered by the waters of the Tagus.

From Toledo the Cardinal Archbishop rules the Roman Catholic Church of Spain in pomp and power which are still almost medieval. His cathedral houses incomparable riches, gold and silver vessels, paintings and vestments, many of them consecrated over four hundred years ago, when Mexico and Peru were pouring wealth into Spain.

Strangely enough, one of the greatest of 'Spanish' painters was a Greek, 'El Greco' as they called him in the land where he became famous. He settled in Toledo, and painted there for forty years, in a house which can still be visited, and many of his paintings are still in Toledo. El Greco was haunted by a strange genius which saw men and women with long, twisted bodies, narrow faces and an unearthly look, often in sickly green-white shades.

Toledo is a maze of narrow streets and little *plazas*

Heavy industry at Bilbao

Industry and Fishing

Spain is a land rich in minerals. Near Huelva in the south is the Rio Tinto, one of the most productive copper regions of the world. Here you can see the river actually running red with its deposits. These mines were worked regularly by the Romans, and by the Carthaginians before them, and are in full employment today.

In the north Bilbao is the focus of much mineral wealth. More than a quarter of a million people live in this chief town of the Basque country. Iron ore is found in the hills behind the coast and is shipped from the quays of Bilbao. Coal is also mined in the north, among the mountains of the Asturias, though it is not easy to transport in this rough and rugged district.

Many large waterpower stations have been built in recent years to provide electricity, by making dams across the east-to-west rivers which flow into Portugal, and also across the Ebro river. These dams have also raised the level of the water, benefiting irrigation.

Despite the expansion of mineral trade, it is still upon the fruit farmer that Spain relies mostly for her national income. The fertile lands of the south form one vast orchard which

Fishing boats at La Escala on the Costa Brava   A fish market near Barcelona

sends oranges, lemons, grapes, apricots, melons and many other fruits to the markets of the world. They are still chiefly cultivated and harvested by hand, which is far more congenial to the Spanish temperament than mechanical work.

The abundance of fresh fish is one of the best features of food in Spain. Fast motor trucks bring catches from the ports to most towns by dawn. Then you will see fish pedlars, with flat boxes of fresh fish strapped on their bicycles, going their rounds from house to house. There is a flourishing sardine trade in Spain (as in neighbouring Portugal) and the north coast is cut by long, deep creeks where lobsters, crabs, crayfish and cuttlefish are caught.

In the south there is a spectacular tuna drive every year in spring and autumn, when thousands of these fish enter and leave the Mediterranean through the Strait of Gibraltar. Nets are stretched at special points, ending in a blind alley. Swarms of tunny, sometimes as many as five hundred, swim into this trap and find themselves surrounded by boats, with no escape. Many of these fish are six feet in length. This is a very ancient practice, since we know that the Spanish sent these tunny for the tables of rich men in Rome in the time of the emperors, some of whom were born in Andalusia.

The walls of
Ávila

Castles
and
Cathedrals

Spain is full of hills and it sometimes seems that almost every hill is crowned by its castle, great or small. In ancient times this was the stronghold of a noble, and round it grew up the life of his city. This is why today the railway stations in Spain are so far from their towns. The castle had to be high. The railway had to be low. Often a couple of dusty miles separate the two.

Frequently a city is dominated by two great buildings – the cathedral and the castle. The latter is usually called by the Moorish name *Alcázar*, just as fortified heights in Greece are called *Acropolis*. Many of these strongholds show marks of storm and siege suffered through the centuries, right down to the Civil War of the 1930s. Some of them, such as the Alcázar of Segovia in Castile, look like great ships riding above the plain. Others have been in past days palaces as well as fortresses, like the Alhambra of Granada. Some of them have changed hands many times, among the warlike nobles who plundered Spain in the Middle Ages. Some of them are now turned into hotels run by the State (called *paradores*), where guests can find lodging in remote regions, such as mountain passes where the castle used to guard an approach to the plains. Spain was one of the first countries in Europe to develop this use for historic buildings which would otherwise have fallen into decay.

Sometimes these castles comprised whole cities, like Ávila, with its ring of walls and turrets, perhaps the finest medieval city left in Europe. Even the cathedral is built into a bastion of its walls. Ávila, standing at nearly 4,000 feet above sea level, is the highest city in Spain. Its walls are fortified at intervals with eighty-six towers and are pierced by ten gateways – a formidable stronghold to storm.

No other country in the world possesses four cathedrals so fine as those of Toledo, Burgos, León and Seville. In addition to these there are more than forty other major ones and a host of minor cathedrals in Spain. Not only are many of them superb in design and fabric, but they are also decorated inside with priceless treasures which the New World poured into Spain in the golden days of the *conquistadores*. Often whole Bible stories are carved in stone, to aid the imagination of simple worshippers who found difficulty in reading the printed word.

Most of these medieval stone masterpieces have been far better preserved in Spain than in harsher climates further north where wind and weather have often caused severe damage to ancient stonework.

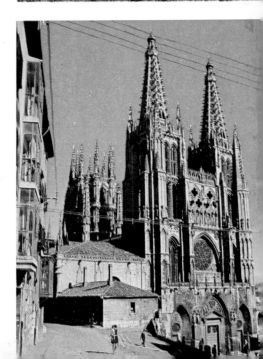

Three great cathedrals:
Seville, Segovia and Burgos

35

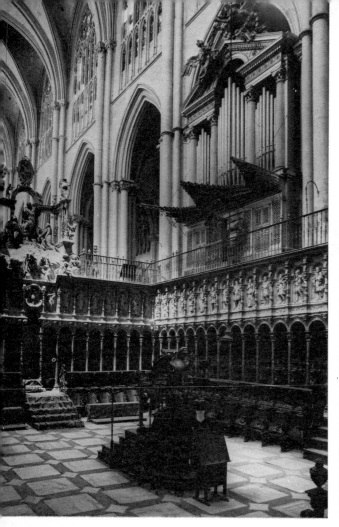

There is one strange feature of Spanish cathedrals. Often a high-walled choir is placed in the middle of the nave, instead of at the east end. This makes it difficult to view the interior as a whole. Sometimes this *coro* is so large that it looks like a church within a church. This also emphasises the width of Spanish cathedrals, in contrast with British and French ones, whose dominating impression is of length and height.

Two other features are outstanding. Gigantic altarpieces – called *retablos* – are common, adorned by the best sculptors and painters of each age. These are not confined to Spain, but are particularly fine there. Even more striking, and essentially

Spanish, are the huge wrought-iron grilles to be found in many churches. The making of these *rejas*, as they are called, often dates from the days when wealth began to flow into Spain from the Americas. Many of these screens are decorated with coats-of-arms. Others are beautifully gilded or silvered. Some of these were preserved in times of danger by being painted black to deceive pillagers. Many Spanish cathedrals were reared on the sites or foundations of earlier shrines. At Seville, for example, Christian builders destroyed the Moorish mosque but had the good taste to leave the superb minaret which still flanks the huge cathedral which they built. The Moors had probably used Roman material in making this Giralda tower, so that three civilizations are represented here.

At Córdoba an even more remarkable event took place. A Christian cathedral has been built right inside the great Moslem mosque. This is still called the Mesquita, and has retained its entirely Moorish character, with its forest of slender columns and its gracefully interwoven horseshoe arches, striped with red brick and white stone. Many of these columns were brought by the Moors from other places such as Carthage and Constantinople. In this shrine gathered the famous leather-workers of Córdoba, the 'cordwainers', whose name still survives in the City of London as the Worshipful Company of Cordwainers. Outside the Mesquita is a courtyard of orange trees with fountains playing under the shadow of the Bell Tower, which now replaces the minaret from which the call to prayer used to go out to the Moslem faithful.

Detail of an altarpiece in Ávila cathedral

37

The Alhambra, Granada

Granada and the Moors

The Moors from North Africa ruled most of Spain for nearly eight centuries after they crossed the Strait of Gibraltar in A.D. 711. Nowhere is their influence more evident than in Granada. The Alhambra on its hill above the city transports the visitor on a magic carpet to Baghdad, to a world of graceful pavilions, cool waters and sweet flowers, conjuring up memories of slaves and sultans, mystery and intrigue. Here is the Court of Lions, the Pool of Myrtles and the sinister Room of Secrets from which enemies of the Arab caliphs might disappear without trace.

Nearby is a garden called the Generalife, a graphic illustration of why the Greek word for garden was 'paradise', for here the Moors took their ease in the hot summer months amid tall

Sacramonte from the Alhambra   The Court of Lions

cypresses, fragrant jasmine and roses, fountains and flower beds.

The Alhambra was the cherished home of the invaders, and their last stronghold in Spain before they were driven out by the troops of Ferdinand and Isabella in 1492. Its massive walls still stand, though Charles V, grandson of Ferdinand and Isabella and the second Hapsburg ruler of Spain, destroyed part of it to build a palace for himself. Mercifully he spared most of its lovely courtyards, its delicately arched and tiled rooms and lofty balconies. The later Hapsburgs kept it in good order, but when the Hapsburg line died out in 1700 and the Bourbon descendants of Louis XIV of France ruled Spain, the Alhambra was allowed to fall into decay and became a den of smugglers and thieves.

Fountains in the gardens of
the Generalife

In 1829 a young American, Washington Irving, fell in love with its grandeur, came to live in it and wrote a series of stories called *Tales of the Alhambra*. This book so charmed Americans and Britons that it brought them flocking to Granada. These early visitors have now been followed by crowds from all over the world.

At the foot of the Alhambra hill stands the cathedral where Ferdinand and Isabella chose to be buried, in a richly decorated chapel. These two monarchs, of Aragon and Castile, united Spain which, until their time, had been a battleground for warring states. Isabella is one of the heroic figures of history, on the scale of Boadicea and Joan of Arc, and her feats of campaigning in a bleak land have become legendary.

Granada is superbly situated 2,000 feet above sea level, with the peaks of the Sierra Nevada rising 11,000 feet in the clear air behind. There are caves in the hills round Granada and here you can watch flamenco dancing. Gaudily dressed men and women whirl and spin, dazzling the eye with the speed of their footwork and assaulting the ear with the intricate rhythms of their castanets, hand

The tomb of Ferdinand of
Aragon and Isabella of Castile

40

The chimney pots of the cave dwellings at Guadix

claps or finger snapping. Some of these caverns are now elaborate dwellings, complete with fashionable furniture, electric light and even telephones. Near Granada, at Guadix, there is a whole settlement of cave dwellers. Here, in a sort of lunar landscape, chimney pots project from mounds of soft tufa rock, and doors in the hillside lead into deep burrows where hundreds of families live in twilight – a human honeycomb.

These cave dwellers are gipsies who swarm all over Andalusia and the next province of Murcia. They came to Spain in the fifteenth century, attracted by its warmth, its fruit, its fine horses and cattle. In early days Spanish law harshly forbade them to take part in trade, and so they led a wandering life, in their cavalcades of brightly painted vans, thieving and plundering. Gradually the laws became milder, and now many of them are settled in communities as in Granada. Some have even given up their gipsy language and dress, but most of them still cling to the strange tribal customs which these Romany folk observe all over Europe. More than a hundred years ago an Englishman called George Borrow wrote a book, *The Gipsies of Spain*, which gives a fascinating picture of their nomadic life.

The *matadores* enter the ring, followed by their teams

The Bull Fight – Plaza de Toros

Early in the evening on Sunday you will see crowds streaming towards the bull ring. All classes in Spain attend the *corrida*. Richer people buy 'shade' tickets and poorer ones 'sun' tickets, because even late in the day the Spanish summer sun can be fierce. The bull fighting season extends from April until autumn.

A president, seated in his special box, controls the ceremony. At his entry, a trumpet sounds and two other officials, wearing sixteenth-century costume, ride across to salute him. Then the three *matadores*, the stars of the performance, appear, followed by their teams. All bow to the president, who throws down the key to the bull pen. The pen is unlocked and the first bull enters the ring.

Six bulls are usually engaged in each *corrida* opposed by three *matadores*, each fighting twice in the evening. Every contest is a three-act drama. First come the *picadores*, on their horses. They goad the bull with long lances, provoking him to charge

42

again and again. Next come the *banderilleros*, attacking with yard-long wooden sticks tipped with steel points. Their duty is to drive into the bull four pairs of these *banderillas* to enrage him and to weaken the muscles of his neck. Then the *matador*, 'the killer', completes the drama.

The dress of the *matador* is very striking. He wears a 'suit of lights' – tight breeches laced at the knee, and a short jacket with wide shoulders, all brightly coloured and encrusted with spangles and small jewels. In the last act, the 'moment of truth', the *matador* faces the bull singlehanded in a contest of which the moves are as clearly defined as the steps of a ballet. If he kills quickly, at a distance, he will be greeted with howls of rage. The test of his skill is to see how near he can draw the bull to himself, with passes of his *muleta* (red cloth), before he goes in over the very horns of the animal to deliver the final thrust. During this phase the bull often rips the heavily embroidered costume of his antagonist, and every bull ring is equipped with a small hospital and chapel to deal with the wounds inevitably inflicted.

The final stages of the bull fight

Bull fighting on horseback. The *matador* is mounted and has to be a superb horseman

Popular *matadores* earn huge fortunes. In the season their life is not only extremely dangerous but very exhausting. They travel all over Spain to perform at important *fiestas*. Some even fly to Mexico, to challenge comparison with the experts there. An outstanding young *matador* is cheered and driven on by his public to spectacular feats until one day he suffers the *cornada* (goring) through working too close to the horns.

Bull rearing for the ring is a profitable industry in Spain. The bull as well as the *matador* must display courage and stamina. A weak or timid bull evokes jeers for himself and often for his adversary too. He is not at all like the large, heavy, slow bull usually bred in other lands. He is agile, tough and wiry. He is also very fast for his half-ton weight and has wicked, curling horns. He is tested at many stages of his upbringing to ensure that he is up to standard. It has been remarked that *matadores* are more often killed by 'bad bulls' than by 'brave bulls'. The former might have, for example, a defect in one eye which causes them to 'hook' to left or right and thus surprise a *matador* who is expecting a straight charge.

44

The bull ring is enclosed by a wooden fence, called the *barrera*. Between this fence and the first row of seats is a passageway, the *callejón*. Here stand the members of the *matador's* team, busy with preparations. In the *barrera* you can see four narrow openings, protected by wooden shields. They are built to admit the body of a man, but not that of a bull, so that a hard-pressed *torero* can seek refuge.

The crowd is very closely identified with the bull fight, quick to give praise and blame. It has often been condemned by Anglo-Saxons as unsporting. No judgment could be more confused. The *corrida* never was a sport. It has always been an elaborate ritual, giving expression to the cruelty and courage combined in the Spanish character. It is a carefully evolved art, governed by complicated rules, presenting a vivid and moving pageant.

The spectators can be very cruel to a *matador* who bungles his job, but they also insist upon rewards for a courageous performance. In this case they urge the president to award an ear or a hoof of the bull to show their pleasure. The *matador* holds these trophies aloft as he jogs round the arena, often being showered by gifts from the crowd as he goes.

This custom has now spread in many lands to football teams, who often run round the ground displaying a cup which they have won.

Small boys playing at bull fighting

45

Cádiz, the port of Seville, through which the wealth of the New World poured into Spain

Springboard for the New World

Some fifty miles southwest of Seville lies the tiny village of Palos. Here, nearly five centuries ago, began one of the most momentous voyages in history.

The Genoese sailor, Christopher Columbus, rejected by his own people, had finally won the support of Isabella of Castile. With three small ships and the help of two local shipowners, Martin and Vicente Pinzón, Columbus set off in August 1492 and reached the New World, firmly believing himself, to the end of his life, that he had found another route to the Indies. This is why the Columbus Library in Seville (begun by his son, Fernando) is named the Archives of the Indies, with no reference to America. Here you may see many relics of the great navigator, including charts and calculations worked out for him by the mathematicians of Salamanca University, which was, in Columbus's time, one of the greatest seats of learning in the world.

Isabella believed in Columbus much more firmly than her husband did; King Ferdinand of Aragon's main care at that time was his victorious campaign against the Moors. Therefore the glory of the four voyages which Columbus made to the West belongs especially to Isabella. By her will only her Castilian subjects were to enjoy the right to trade and settle in the Indies.

The ancient port of Palos has changed out of all knowledge in the passage of years. In the time of Columbus the sea flowed to the doors of its cottages. Now the land has silted up and meadows cover what was then its port. But you can still see the ancient fountain from which the explorers filled their water casks. You can also see, overgrown by grass, a row of rusty rings to which the *Santa Maria*, the *Niña* and the *Pinta* may once have been moored.

The little monastery of La Rabida at Palos overlooks the mouth of the Rio Tinto. It was here that Columbus found shelter and comfort in the weary time of waiting and discouragement. He left his young son in this monastery to be taught and cared for while he was at sea. The abbot of La Rabida pleaded the cause of Columbus before Queen Isabella, whose confessor he had been in earlier days. In those days he ruled a rich and flourishing community of forty monks. Now there is only a handful, to welcome strangers and point out to them the huge Columbus statue across the estuary. They also guard and proudly display a score of little boxes, made of many different kinds of wood, containing soil sent by the republics of South America to rest at the shrine of their origin.

A reconstruction of Columbus's ship can be seen in the harbour at Barcelona

The old tobacco factory in Seville

Seville and Holy Week

Seville is the great city of Andalusia, and ranks as the capital of southern Spain. Its cathedral, second only to St Peter's at Rome in size, is one of the most magnificent in Christendom. Above it rises the lofty Giralda bell tower, built by the Moors to match others which they built at Marrakesh and Rabat in Morocco.

Seville is rich in churches. Many of them possess elaborately carved figures which are carried through the streets on the Thursday before Good Friday. Between the figures are carried tableaux depicting the last days of Jesus on earth. No wheels are visible beneath the platforms; their beams are fitted with yokes for the shoulders of the bearers, part of their Lenten penance. From each parish church a procession of some two hundred penitents sets out, walking in deathly silence, wearing high conical head-dresses that mask their faces.

Many of the groups bear an image of the Virgin, wearing a halo of jewel-studded gold and robes of richest silk. The most popular of her statues is the Virgin of Hope, called *La Macarena* from the quarter where she lives, in Triana, the gipsy suburb of Seville. *La Macarena* is the guardian of poor people and of bullfighters, many of whom make valuable offerings at her shrine, seeking her protection.

Suddenly in the silence you hear a high-pitched wailing note, a song of lamentation, called a *saeta* (from the Latin *sagitta*), an 'arrow of prayer' shot straight from earth to heaven. These wild chants are part of the dark pomp of Our Lord's death. The people of Spain have never sought to disguise the cruel death which Jesus suffered on the Cross. Every crucifix in the land, vividly carved and painted, is a similar reminder. The scene in Holy Week is grim and somewhat terrifying, but it is designed to remind people that it was through torture and death that Christ redeemed the world.

Behind the processions walk priests in their vestments, and attendants swinging censers. After these surge vast crowds, heading for the cathedral which is the hub of this dramatic scene. All mourning ends with Good Friday. Easter Saturday is given over to wild rejoicing, as the people abandon restraint after the long fast of Lent. People flock from all over the world to the pageant of Holy Week, and every room in Seville is crammed with guests.

La Amargura, the Virgin of Sorrows, one of the statues carried through Seville in Holy Week

The great *Feria* or fair of Seville takes place in late April. A whole town of small pavilions or *casetas*, decorated with flowers and chains of bright lights, springs up. In these Sevillian families entertain their friends and watch the night-long dancing and merrymaking. The origin of the *casetas* is traced

LEFT A courtyard
RIGHT A street
during the Feria

to the tents pitched by cattle dealers so that they could sleep near their herds to protect them from thieves.

Hundreds of riders parade, dressed in the handsome regional costume of Andalusia, the men in leather trousers, short jackets and hard, wide brimmed hats and the girls, perched behind them or seated in carriages, in gay flounced dresses. During the six days of the Fair, Seville sleeps little. Life is a round of visits to the sound of guitar and castanets.

Seville is a city of typically Andalusian charm. It has winding streets and lanes enclosed by high walls, linking little squares with rose gardens surrounded by gaily tiled seats. Some streets are so narrow that vehicles are forbidden. In summer awnings are stretched by day to keep out the fierce sun, and at night the canvas is furled so that you may sit under the sky.

Windows are screened with iron grilles and brightly painted shutters. Courtyards give glimpses of clematis and geranium tumbling round doorways and of golden oranges. In spring the scent of orange blossom fills the air. Yet the chief delight of Seville is its people who have the good looks and grace for which Spanish men and women are famous. You will find in Seville the perfection of manners and good taste which the mingling of East and West has given to the southern parts of Spain.

Education

Education has a long history in Spain. During the Moorish domination schools were founded in great numbers; in Córdoba, which was then as famous for learning as Rome, Athens or Byzantium, one Arab ruler endowed no less than twenty-seven. When the Moors left Spain, the Roman Catholic Church played a leading part in education for many centuries.

The years since the end of the Civil War have marked a rapid expansion in schooling all over Spain. There are still remote regions where it is hard to compel attendance, but by law all Spanish children are required to stay at school till the age of fourteen, and severe penalties are laid down for both employers and parents if any young person is offered a job without producing the certificate of education awarded only to those who remain at school till that age.

Spanish children outside their school

In the primary schools reading, writing, history, religious knowledge and elementary mathematics are the main subjects. Children who pass the test for high school entry transfer from their primary schools at the age of ten and begin a six-year period of study with a wider curriculum, including science and foreign languages; French and English are the two usually chosen. Organized games are not played in Spanish schools, but most boys are keen soccer players and make up their own teams among their friends. The summer holidays are long, as in other European countries, from mid-July to mid-September, and the winter holidays are short.

At sixteen an examination is held to decide which pupils are suitable for university training. These then take a one-year pre-university course and can, if they are clever, reach university at seventeen. Many, however, have to take the course two or three times and so do not begin their university studies until they are eighteen or nineteen.

Education at university level is expanding just as fast as at school level. Two new establishments in Madrid and Barcelona are now being added to the large ones already existing in those cities. Spain's tradition of university education is a very old one dating back to A.D. 1230 when the university of Salamanca was founded, and it has spread to other countries too, for one must not forget the scores of universities which Spaniards have founded in the New World – in Buenos Aires, Mexico, Lima, Santiago de Chile and in many other great cities.

Spanish students in eighteenth-century costume seranading the girls of Jerez de la Frontera

Farming

Pumping water

In most parts of Spain peasant families still farm their land by methods which their fathers have used for centuries. Threshing in particular looks almost as it must have done in Biblical days, as the grain is pressed down on the threshing floor by wooden sledges driven round by oxen or mules.

The olive harvest marks an important milestone in the farmer's year. When the olives have been gathered and dried in the sun, they are pressed in a stone mill, usually worked by a donkey. Then the crushed olives are allowed to stand for some weeks so that the dregs can settle before the pure oil on top is drained off.

Maize is grown in clumps wherever there is enough soil in hilly regions. After harvest the farmers decorate their houses with its golden bunches, hanging them from the balconies to dry.

In the south, particularly round Valencia, rice fields, sugar cane and orange groves abound. The latter are a fascinating sight between October and April, the months of picking. So well have methods of spreading the harvest been developed that in spring you may see late fruit and early blossom

Harvesting cotton near Córdoba

hanging on the trees at the same time. The season which the farmer fears is January, when a sudden frost may ruin his crops. This is rare, happily.

This is a rich countryside, with reddish soil. Irrigation is the main problem, because without ample moisture all fruit would quickly wither and die. Methods of watering, by wells and connecting trenches, shaded by palms and carob trees, have been handed down almost unchanged from the days of the Moorish occupation. Water rights are jealously guarded by the farmers, and even their small children take part in building the little dams which control its flow. So vital is irrigation that a Water Court has met once a week for a thousand years in Valencia, to try cases when anyone is accused of wasting water, and to settle disputes.

The Pyrenean farmer by contrast has very different problems. Although the soil is stony, except in deep valleys, he has plenty of rain. He has to contend with late springs and long winters during which he turns to woodcutting when his fields are lying under snow.

Drying maize

One problem which faces the farmer in most of Spain is erosion – the wearing away of the soil by rain, high winds and the lack of vegetation. The sheep and goats which graze everywhere add to the trouble by cropping all young shoots. This danger is now well realized, and in bare regions trees are being planted to hold the soil.

The vintage festival at Jerez, when the first grapes are pressed

Most people in the region around Jerez in southern Spain earn their living making the golden wine which has been popular in Britain for centuries. Today almost three-quarters of Spain's sherry is exported to Britain.

Jerez itself is a town of more than a 100,000 inhabitants. It is built of an ochre, sherry-tinted stone, and is the home of solid warehouses, called *bodegas*, enclosing cool courtyards shaded by palms, lemon trees and acacias. Here the wine is stored, bottled and then dispatched all over the world. Inside the *bodegas* great oak casks containing more than a hundred gallons are banked in three tiers. When sherry is sold it is taken from the bottom row of casks which are then replenished from the ones above. Thus the older wine is being constantly blended with the younger, and is not kept strictly in vintages like other wines.

Regular testing is important. For this, a thin rod with a tiny silver cup is let down into the cask. Through this a sample is drawn and poured into a little tulip-shaped glass. The expert tests this more through sense of smell than taste. There is great variety in the taste and appearance of sherry, from a very heavy, deep-

Making barrels

brown, sweet wine to a pale, almost greeny-yellow dry one.

Around Jerez lie miles of vineyards in which sherry grapes are grown. Young vines are planted in holes about six feet deep and two feet square, filled with loose earth and rubble. These are dug to preserve moisture because there is no rainfall in the whole of the late spring and summer. In September when the vintage comes the large white grapes are gathered and brought into the farms on carts drawn by oxen. Rush mats are spread in the yards where the grapes are exposed to the burning sun. This is called the *soleado*. This makes them over-ripe and the longer they lie the greater their sugar content. Twenty-four hours is sufficient for a dry wine, but up to two weeks is required for a very sweet one. After this the grapes are shovelled into huge wooden vats. Men shod in leather boots with nailed soles then tread them out, just as they did in Roman times. The craft of sherry making has been handed down, exact in every detail, for generations among the families of Jerez.

Many other countries now make and export 'sherry', but none of them has yet succeeded in matching the taste of real Jerez sherry.

Inside the *bodega*

The North

Basque houses

The Basque people who live in the north of Spain are a tough, sturdy, independent race. There are Spanish Basques and French Basques. Despite the frontier running between them they feel a great sense of kinship and have a language in common. They are athletic and energetic, great eaters and drinkers. Like many who live among mountains the Basques are thickset and stocky and can keep going for hours on the rough tracks of their hills. They build handsome wooden houses, of a distinctive pattern, not unlike the chalets found in the Alps.

Their neighbours on the east inhabit the former kingdom of Navarre. Through their land runs the ancient highway which crosses the Pyrenees at the Pass of Roncesvalles. Here, in A.D. 778, the great knight Roland was slain, covering the retreat of the Emperor Charlemagne, battling against the Moors. This was also the pilgrims' way in the Middle Ages for devout people journeying to Santiago de Compostela to the shrine of St James, patron saint of Spain. The men of Navarre, like those of Aragon next to them, were renowned warriors in the days when all these regions were split up into rival kingdoms.

To the west of the Basques lie Asturias and Galicia. The Asturian mountains are wild and desolate, with fierce winters. The Moorish invaders never penetrated this region, and it was from this stronghold that the Christian reconquest was launched.

When you leave Asturias and enter Galicia, you become aware at once that you are in a different region, with moors, low hills, marshes and white cottages. It has often been compared with Ireland, and there is something in the bearing of the people too, as well as in the moist and misty climate of their green fields, that recalls the Irish.

A cape on the west coast of Galicia is called Finisterre, 'world's end', which it truly was before the discovery of the New World. The two great harbours of Vigo and La Coruña, with safe anchorages and crowded quaysides, largely trade with the western hemisphere, and many emigrants still leave from here for the voyage across the Atlantic to the Americas to find greater prosperity than their own bare hillsides can offer.

Santa Cilia de Jaca in the Pyrenees

Playing *pelota*

Sport

In recent years *El Futbol* has made great strides in Spain. Most cities support a first-class soccer team. The Real (Royal) Madrid team have often been European champions and make frequent tours in South America. Some fine golf courses have been laid out since World War II, particularly in the south, but golf is still a rich man's game in Spain.

The most distinctively local game is *pelota* which has the reputation of being the fastest and most exhausting ball game in the world. *Pelota* originated as an open air sport on both sides of the Pyrenees, among the athletic Basques, but it is regularly played as a court game in big cities such as Madrid and Barcelona. It is even played as far afield as Mexico, Cuba and the United States, though the best performers are almost always Basques.

In *pelota* the players sometimes use bare hands, but more usually they strap on to their hands a wickerwork scoop called a *chistera* or *cesta*. With this they catch a hard ball and sling it at high speed against a wall called the *fronton*. This is some thirty feet high and fifty wide. Often this wall is provided by the village church and the priest can sometimes be seen hitching up his cassock to join in the game. Back from this wall runs the court, into which the ball rebounds great distances. Much skill is required to catch the ball and to sustain the rallies, and players have to be young and extremely fit. All the force of the body follows the mighty swing with which the ball is delivered. In country districts *pelota* is chiefly played for exercise and entertainment, but in cities it is a source of heavy gambling. Brisk betting accompanies the course of a game, as the shouts of bookmakers mingle with the cries of spectators.

Yacht racing is popular round the coasts of Spain, very fittingly for a country which provided in Juan Sebastian El Cano, Magellan's lieutenant, the first man to sail round the world after the latter's death in the Pacific, nearly sixty years before the voyage of Francis Drake. Rowing regattas are also held regularly at seaside resorts such as San Sebastian, Santander and La Coruña in the north. Here the boats are not shell-thin craft such as you see in river racing, but stout and tough to resist the force of waves, and they are steered not by a delicate rudder but by a captain plying a long oar from the stern.

A regatta at La Coruña

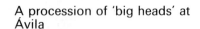

Fiestas

The Spanish year is gay with *fiestas* or feast days. Some are religious, such as the elaborate processions which mark Corpus Christi Day each summer, when statues of the Virgin are carried through the streets, and the crowds kneel at her passing. Other festivals are gay and mocking, such as the *Fallas* of Valencia, when huge *papier-mâché* figures of well-known people are erected in the streets. Spaniards love these giants and the 'big heads' which enliven many of their holidays. The *Romería del Rocío* is a famous Andalusian festival. The people travel in decorated ox carts and on horseback to the shrine of Our Lady of the Dew at El Rocío, camping on the

The Romeria of St Isidore in Tenerife in the Canary Islands

The Romería del Rocío. LEFT The pilgrimage to the shrine.
RIGHT The pilgrims crowd round the statue of the Virgin, trying
to touch it

way. It is something between a pilgrimage and a picnic. There
is religious fervour when the statue of the Virgin is brought
out from its shrine and there are processions of horsemen and
dancing and singing too, and the encampments at night are
bright with fires, with laughter and the strumming of guitars.

Many *fiestas* are linked with the great religious houses, such as
Poblet near Tarragona, the richest in Europe until it was
sacked by a mob in the last century, and the local saint's day
brings the country people together to celebrate far into the
warm night with fireworks, feasting and song.

No *fiesta* is complete without dancing. Many people think
that Spanish dancing consists entirely of *flamenco*, but this is
not so as every region has its own dances, costume and
music – for instance, the *sardana* in Catalonia, the *jota* in
Aragon and Navarre, the *sevillanas* in Seville – each with its
distinctive footwork and arm movements. Dancing was in the
people's blood long before Spanish dancing girls enchanted
their Roman overlords two thousand years ago.

Index

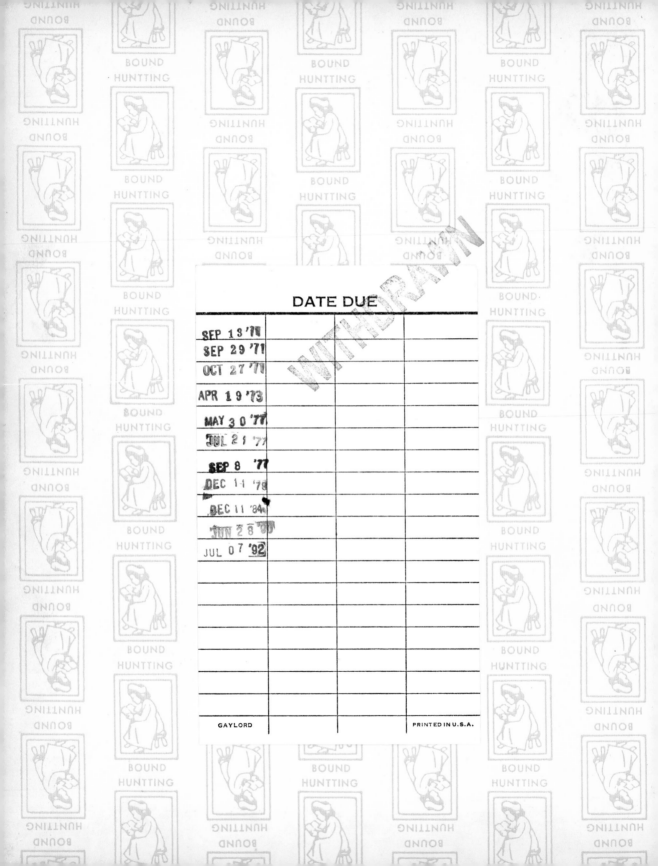